Daddy's Girl

Copyright © 2014 Sue Young
All rights reserved.

For performance fees and enquiries, contact
steveyoungwork@hotmail.com

CAST

Dad
Daughter
Alter Ego
Crooner/Abacus

Only four actors are required. Each main character plays all other minor roles. If required, separate actors can take on the roles of Crooner and Abacus.

Alter Ego - also takes the character of the Mad Axe Man, The Gypsy and The Prostitute
Dad - also plays the role of Mr. Nice and The Swindler
Daughter - also plays the character of Mrs Nice
Crooner - also takes on the role of The Heckler and Abacus.

A widowed father is possessive of his only daughter and his fear of loneliness makes him use every trick in the book to keep her with him. Although she needs to be free of his emotional ties, the daughter doesn't have the heart to leave him. Along comes Alter Ego, a dynamic woman, just dying to burst out of the daughters imagination. All it takes, is a little push to make her dreams a reality. As the Alter Ego and the Daughter become one, the woman she always dreamed of, is born. She walks away, into her new life, leaving a few surprises in her wake.

Daddy's Girl was commissioned and performed by Kirkby Response Theatre. It came second in 'Top Ten Plays of 1992' in an arts review. As with the authors debut play, 'Theatre Wrecks', 'Daddy's Girl' received a standing ovation on the final night of the tour.

Running Time - approximately 1 hour.

The set consists of a large flowered armchair, centre stage, with a standing lamp on one side and a T.V table on the other which holds a remote control, tobacco, pipe and framed photograph. There is a larger table upstage, behind the chair, sturdy enough for two people to sit on. A full length mirror frame stands to the left, slightly upstage.

DADDY'S GIRL

(ENTER DAUGHTER. THE SONG 'WANG,WANG BLUES', by HENRY BUSSE, BEGINS. SHE WALKS TOWARDS A FULL LENGTH MIRROR FRAME.
ENTER ALTER EGO WHO BECOMES THE DAUGHTERS REFLECTION.
THEY COPY EACH OTHER MOVEMENTS. WHEN THE MUSIC STOPS, THE DAUGHTER TWIRLS AWAY FROM THE MIRROR. THE ALTER EGO TURNS IN THE OPPOSITE DIRECTION AND EXITS. THE MUSIC STOPS. ENTER DAD)

DAD: Slippers!

DAUGHTER: I go looking for his slippers but they don't want to know.

DAD: Slippers!

DAUGHTER: I can see them trembling under the table. 'Don't put me on his feet again tonight. We couldn't stand it! But I tell them to be brave.

DAD: Tea!

DAUGHTER: Tea is what you drink when the whole world is

falling apart.

DAD: Pipe!

DAUGHTER: And I run for the pipe like there's no tomorrow.

DAD: Dream!

DAUGHTER: And I dream like there's no tomorrow.

DAD: I'm out!

DAUGHTER: And he's out...like there's no tomorrow.

DAD: I'd take you to the pub love, only I don't want them all sitting there, talking through their beer bellies, thinking, 'She's a bit too young for him!'

DAUGHTER: I took up where mum left off. I told her I'd never end up like her, yet here I am, doing for dad what she did for him.

DAD: Supper!

DAUGHTER: It's at times like this, when his tobacco runs out and the football's on the telly, that I just wish I could run away...and when the night time comes...

DAD: Goodnight love.

DAUGHTER: I turn out the light, listen to him snoring...and let my imagination take control...

(DAUGHTER WALKS TO THE MIRROR. ENTER ALTER EGO, WHO APPEARS AS THE REFLECTION. THE DAUGHTER ADMIRES HER FIGURE AND CLOTHES,

TURNS HER BACK ON THE MIRROR AND WALKS AWAY. THE ALTER EGO WALKS THROUGH THE MIRROR AND TAPS THE DAUGHTER ON THE SHOULDER)

ALTER EGO: You haven't got the guts to leave him have you?

DAUGHTER: He'd die without me.

ALTER EGO: Leave him.

DAUGHTER: I would but he's not just any man.

ALTER EGO: No, he's worse.

DAUGHTER: I haven't been in this situation for very long.

ALTER EGO: Only five years.

DAUGHTER: I'm still young.

ALTER EGO: Young enough to fly.

DAUGHTER: I'll leave him soon.

ALTER EGO: When?

DAD: Breakfast!

(EXIT ALTER EGO)

DAUGHTER: A scratch of the balls, a quick fart, then the mouth opens like a baby bird.

DAD: Talking to yourself again.

DAUGHTER: I'm going to work.

DAD: Looking like that? (HE PRODUCES A TAPE MEASURE AND MEASURES HER SKIRT) An inch shorter and you'd have been in trouble. All right, you just about pass.

DAUGHTER: One of these days I'm going to shock him.

DAD: Don't forget to darn my socks.

DAUGHTER: But they're more hole than sock. Why don't I just get you some new ones?

DAD: There's nothing wrong with them!

DAUGHTER: I should throw them away.

DAD: Don't you dare. There's too much of this throwing away business these days. You don't know you're born. I'm lucky to have socks with holes.

DAUGHTER: Don't worry, I'll mend 'em.

DAD: Oh? Is that the post I just heard through the door?

DAUGHTER: I'll kiss the postman.

DAD: Have you brought the milk in?

DAUGHTER: I'll ravage the milkman.

DAD: Don't forget to pay the insurance man.

DAUGHTER: And as for the insurance man...

(ENTER ALTER EGO)

ALTER EGO: Take things step by step. Save the insurance man for when you get out of this prison.

DAUGHTER: I wish.

ALTER EGO: Don't wish.

DAUGHTER: Wish I could...

ALTER EGO: Don't wish. Just go.

DAUGHTER: I can't.

DAD: Moon.

DAUGHTER: (PAUSE) And then one day, he asked me for the moon.

DAD: Moon!

DAUGHTER: I can't give him what he wants any more. He's asking too much.

ALTER EGO: Do you know how far away the moon is?

DAUGHTER: Miles and miles and...

ALTER EGO: Leave the old bastard.

DAUGHTER: But I can't. I mean I don't think I should.

ALTER EGO: Don't procrastinate! Stop putting it off. Get out, before it's too late.

DAUGHTER: (PAUSE. CLEARS THROAT): Er...dad?

DAD: What?

DAUGHTER: I'd like to go out tonight.

DAD: What?

ALTER EGO: Speak up.

DAD: Speak up girl. You won't get heard if you don't speak up.

DAUGHTER: I want to go out, so you'll have to get your own tea tonight.

DAD: What?

DAUGHTER: Well, it's all ready. It's a salad. You don't have to cook anything.

DAD: That's right, just throw my meals at me. You just go out and enjoy yourself. Don't worry about me. It doesn't matter that I don't know where you put anything.

DAUGHTER: Well, the kitchen's sort of...out there.

DAD: Don't be funny with me young lady. I...er...I don't feel too good today.

DAUGHTER: I'm still going out.

DAD: Who with?

DAUGHTER: Friends.

DAD: Male or female?

DAUGHTER: It; doesn't matter.

DAD: I'm not having you pregnant.

DAUGHTER: Chance would be a fine thing.

DAD: What? You wash your mouth out with soap!

DAUGHTER: Okay.

DAD: Where are you going?

DAUGHTER: To buy some soap.

(DAD CLUTCHES AT HIS CHEST AND SEEMS TO HAVE

DIFFICULTY BREATHING. THE DAUGHTER TURNS ROUND AND HE REACHES OUT TO HER, AS IF IN PAIN. THE ALTER EGO STANDS BEHIND HIM KNOWINGLY. SHE FOLDS HER ARMS AND ROLLS HER EYES, FED UP WITH HIS LITTLE ROUTINES)

DAUGHTER: (RUSHES OVER TO HELP HIM) Dad? Don't try to get up. It's all right. I'm here. Do you want me to get a doctor?

DAD: (QUICKLY): No love. No need for that. Stay with me. Just stay with me and everything will be okay.

DAUGHTER: Okay dad. Anything you say.

DAD: You won't go out tonight, will you?

DAUGHTER: Not if you're feeling unwell.

DAD: I think I might be. So, you're best staying with me, just in case it happens again.

DAUGHTER: Okay dad.

ALTER EGO: (MIMMICKS): Okay dad. (WHISPERS IN DAUGHTERS EAR) Stand up for yourself.

DAUGHTER: I've got to be nice to him. He might get pain in his chest.

ALTER EGO: It's nice to be nice, except for the person who is nice, then it's not so nice for them. Ever heard the story of Mr and Mrs Nice? They lived in a nice house, with a nice garden and they had nice children.

(DAUGHTER AND DAD BECOME MR AND MRS NICE)

MRS NICE: Hello sweetheart.

MR NICE: Hello honey.

MRS NICE: Have my seat.

MR NICE: Thank you.

MRS NICE: No, let me thank you.

MR.NICE: No, it's my pleasure.

MRS.NICE: What's on television tonight?

MR.NICE: Don't know dear. I'll look in the TV Guide. Ooh, I want to watch the news.

MRS NICE: I want to watch the soaps.

MR.NICE: It's all right love. You watch the soaps.

MRS. NICE: No, you watch the news.

MR. NICE: No, I want you to watch the soaps.

MRS. NICE: Oh, there's someone at the door.

MR. NICE: I'll get the door.

MRS. NICE: No, I'll get the door.

MR. NICE: No-

TOGETHER: We'll both get the door.

MRS. NICE: Oh look, it's a mad axe man.

MR.NICE: Oh so it is dear.

(THE ALTER EGO BECOMES THE AXE MAN, WEILDS AN AXE AND FREEZES)

MRS. NICE: Oh look, our nice children have just had their heads chopped off by the mad axe man.

MR.NICE: That wasn't very nice was it?

MRS. NICE: No, it certainly wasn't.

AXE MAN: It was an accident.

MRS. NICE: Oh, it was an accident.

MR.NICE: Oh, if it was an accident, then you must be awfully shaken.

AXE MAN: I am rather.

MR.NICE: Let's make him a nice cup of tea.

ALTER EGO: And then the mad axe man killed them both.

DAUGHTER: What a lovely story.

ALTER EGO: So don't be nice. It doesn't pay.

DAUGHTER: No. You just get your head chopped off by a mad axeman.

ALTER EGO: Or the passage of time.

DAD: Iron a shirt for us love. There's a good girl. I'm going to go out for a pint tonight. Tape us the football while I'm out.

DAUGHTER: But I was going to go out. I need to get out of this house, out of this life. It smells of pipe smoke and detergent and...yesterday's soup.

DAD: What?

DAUGHTER: I don't want to nag you dad, but I'm not your wife, I'm your daughter.

DAD: What?

DAUGHTER: Can't you say anything except what?

DAD: What? You're not too old to go over my knee.

DAUGHTER: Yes, I am. Dad...don't you dare.

DAD: Where's my slipper?

DAUGHTER: You're mad.

(DAD TAKES UP A SLIPPER AND BEGINS TO STALK HER)

DAD: Come here.

DAUGHTER: At least I got you out of your chair. I thought you were stuck to it.

DAD: Cheek! The fourth commandment, honour thy mother and thy father.

DAUGHTER: I wish I could honour my mother. I'd never honour you!

(DAD SITS DOWN. PICKS UP THE PAPER AND STARTS READING)

DAD: I understand that you are in this mood due to PMT or some such female thing, related to you irrational emotional outbursts, so

I'll just let that last comment drop. Think yourself lucky girl. You're not going out until you get some respect for me.

DAUGHTER: You make it sound like something you buy in the shops.

ALTER EGO: Don't back down now.

DAUGHTER: I shouldn't have spoken to him like that. He's got a bad heart.

ALTER EGO: Yeah, it's funny how it gets bad every time you decide to go out.

DAD: Er...do us a favour love.

DAUGHTER: Yes dad, I know, quarter finals of the F.A Cup. I'll tape it.

DAD: You're a good one, do you know that? You're just like your mother.

DAUGHTER: Yes, I know, that's the problem.

ALTER EGO: Leave him.

DAUHTER: No.

ALTER EGO: We've had this conversation before. So you're just going to sit here and waste away? Listen to me, listen to yourself. Talk to him.

(DAD SWITCHES ON THE SONG 'BEAUTIFUL DREAMER' BY STEPHEN FOSTER. HE PICKS UP THE FRAMED

PHOTOGRAPH AND LOOKS AT IT FONDLY)

DAUGHTER: Dad? I need to talk to you.

DAD: (STILL STARING AT THE PHOTO, LOST IN HIS OWN WORLD)

DAUGHTER: Dad?

(DAD BREAKS DOWN, PUTS HIS HEAD IN HIS HANDS AND STARTS TO CRY QUIETLY)

(DAUGHTER RUNS TO COMFORTS DAD) Oh dad!

DAD: Do you realise it's been five years since she passed away? It feels like a lifetime. Will you look at her, will you look at how her eyes sparkled when she laughed. (DAUGHTER SMILES) I miss her.

DAUGHTER: Me too.

ALTER EGO: Hey!

DAD: (PAUSE) You look a lot like her. Same eyes, same smile.

DAUGHTER: (TO ALTER EGO) Shhh! Not now. (TO DAD) You used to dance to this song didn't you?

DAD: Aye, we did. I used to sing this to you when you were a baby and I would dance with your mother at the same time. So, I took took care of both my girls. (PROUDLY) I was the original multi-tasker.

(DAUGHTER LAUGHS)

I miss dancing to this. (PAUSE) Would you dance with me?

DAUGHTER: What? Now?

DAUGHTER: Yes now.

(THEY BEGIN TO DANCE)

(EXIT ALTER EGO IN A HUFF)

DAD: (SINGS): 'Beautiful dreamer, queen of my song, list while I woe thee with soft melody. Gone are the cares of life's busy throng. Beautiful dreamer, awake unto me. Beautiful dreamer, awake unto me'.

DAUGHTER: Dad?

DAD: Yes love.

DAUGHTER: Can I talk to you about something?

DAD: Sure, any time, what's bothering my little girl?

DAUGHTER: It's my life.

DAD: Your life? What's wrong with it?

DAUGHTER: Nothing happens. I work at the supermarket. I come home. I do the laundry. I cook. I clean. I get your pipe and slippers, I tape your programmes when you're at the pub.

DAD: That sounds like a lot of things happening.

DAUGHTER: I knew you wouldn't understand.

DAD: You've got a nice life. What more do you want?

DAUGHTER: I want people.

DAD: People are more trouble than they're worth. You don't want people. They'll only hurt you. Stay with your old dad. Just you and me eh? You'll be safe with me.

DAUGHTER: I'm not sure I want to be safe.

DAD: I remember the day I got you that managers job at the supermarket. I had a talk to old Fred. Do you remember? I had to pull some strings to get it for you, I can tell you.

DAUGHTER: Yes dad, I know and I'm grateful, but at the same time, I had the qualifications.

DAD: How can you be lonely? You meet people at the shop.

DAUGHTER: Yes but they're customers. I need friendships.

DAD: Well, your friends come around sometimes. You sit in the front room and talk.

DAUGHTER: Then you play your Tammy Wynette records at full volume and they all leave.

(DAD STOPS DANCING AND PULLS AWAY)

DAD: Now, don't you bring Tammy into all this. What's your friends name, the one with the red hair? She said she likes Tammy.

DAUGHTER: She was being polite. (TURNS AWAY) Listen dad, I'm not talking about friends, not of the female kind anyway.

DAD: Ah, I see what it is we're talking about here. Boys right?

DAUGHTER: Men, actually.

DAD: Well, I can tell you all you need to know about boys and more.

DAUGHTER: No, I'm a woman, so I need a man.

DAD: You wash your mouth out with soap! You're making yourself sound cheap. Need men indeed. There are lots of things I could tell you about men.

DAUGHTER: And warm bus seats I suppose.

DAD: What?

DAUGHTER: Nothing.

DAD: As I was saying, there's a lot of bad things I could tell you about men. But we'll talk about this another time. Right now, I'll think I'll have a nap. Wake me up when it's tea time.(HE STARTS TO DOZE)

ALTER EGO: I told you the softly-softly approach doesn't work. You've got to use the proverbial knee in the groin approach.

DAUGHTER: Go away.

ALTER EGO: Start an argument.

DAUGHTER: What?

ALTER EGO: Do something, you silly cow.

DAD: Who are you talking to?

ALTER EGO: Your mother's dead and now he's using you.

(DAUGHTER GASPS)

The truth hurts.

(ALTER EGO APPROACHES DAD. HE DOZES THROUGH HER DIALOGUE)

Hello dad. I'm going out tonight. It looks like you'll have to get your own tea. I think you should have a stew. I've left some vegetables. All you need now is some stock, something that will add flavour to the soup, so I got a pair of your socks from the laundry basket. Just put them in the pan and bring to the boil.

DAUGHTER: Stop it!

ALTER EGO: Do you like what I'm wearing dad? You don't think it's too short do you? Well, I'll wear it anyway. Short skirts are always in aren't they? Oh and by the way, I might stay out all night.

DAUGHTER: Shut up, he might hear you.

ALTER EGO: That's the whole point. (PICKS UP THE PIPE AND GOES TO SMOKE IT)

DAUGHTER: All right, all right. You win. I'll talk to him. (TAKES A DEEP BREATH)

ALTER EGO: Well go on then.

DAUGHTER: I will. (TAKES ANOTHER DEEP BREATH) Dad? (DAD DOESN'T EVEN STIR)

ALTER EGO: Louder.

DAUGHTER: (SHOUTS): Dad?

(DAD WAKES UP IN ALARM): What? Where's the fire?

DAUGHTER: There's no fire.

DAD: You nearly gave me a heart attack.

DAUGHTER: You see dad, I want something.

DAD: What do you want?

DAUGHTER: I want...what I want is...what I want is...to make a nice steak for tea.

DAD: Oh, lovely girl, that sounds lovely.

(DAUGHTER TURNS AWAY DEFEATED)

I like steak but if you'd rather we had something else?

(DAUGHTER TAKES ANOTHER DEEP BREATH AND TURNS ROUND TO FACE DAD)

DAUGHTER: You know what you are?

DAD: What?

ALTER EGO: Full of steaming dog poo.

DAUGHTER: Full of...You're a first class bully, not second, or third, but first.

ALTER EGO: At least he's come first in something.

DAUGHTER: I can't stand your guts and I'm leaving. (LONG PAUSE) He hasn't said very much has he?

ALTER EGO: Let it sink in. (ALTER EGO HANDS DAUGHTER

A SUITCASE)

DAUGHTER: If you'll excuse me, I have some packing to do.

DAD: (CLUTCHING CHEST) Aahhh! It's got me. The old tickers finally got me! Can't take much more...and it's all because of you, my only daughter. (GASPS): In my dying breath, let me just say...aahhh...that a father's worst way to die must be this...while his daughter stands by, watching coldly.

(HE FALLS ON THE FLOOR AND IS STILL)

DAUGHTER: (PAUSE. UNEASILY): Pass me my clothes.

ALTER EGO: The time has come for you to stand up...

DAUGHTER: Jeans.

ALTER EGO: ...and be counted.

DAUGHTER: Shoes

ALTER EGO: It's a new age...

DAUGHTER: Bras

ALTER EGO: ...of the thinking woman.

DAUGHTER: Knickers!

(THE ALTER EGO HELPS THE DAUGHTER CLOSE THE SUITCASE. THEY SIT ON THE TABLE, SWINGING THEIR FEET)

DAUGHTER: Do you know what I think?

ALTER EGO: What?

DAUGHTER: I think he's dead.

ALTER EGO: He's pretending to be dead.

DAUGHTER: (PAUSE) Are you sure?

ALTER EGO: Yes, he always does. You said so yourself. (SIMULTANEOUSLY THE ALTER EGO AND THE DAUGHTER GET DOWN FROM THE TABLE, LEAN FORWARD TO LOOK AT THE DAD, PUT THEIR HAND TO THEIR MOUTH, WRING THEIR HANDS AND EXCHANGE A GLANCE)

DAUGHTER: He's been pretending for a long time hasn't he?

ALTER EGO: Yeah. He should be an actor.

DAUGHTER: Come on dad, you can get up now. (PAUSE) Look I know you're not happy but the least you can do is wish me good luck. Dad? It's not going to work.

(SHE APROACHES THE BODY TENTATIVELY, KNEELS DOWN AND WHISPERS): Dad?

(SHE SHAKES HIM GENTLY) Oh no! (SHAKES HIM MORE VIGOUROUSLY) No...he can't be...

(DAUGHTER BREAKS DOWN)

(ALTER EGO MAKES THE SIGN OF THE CROSS)

I'm sorry dad. I'm so sorry. (SHE LAYS HER HEAD BY HIS FEET. THE DAD SLOWLY SITS UP AND STARES AT THE

DAUGHTER, WHO IS STILL CRYING BY HIS FEET)

DAD: You'll be even more sorry if you don't get that tea on!

(DAUGHTER AND ALTER EGO BOTH START IN SURPRISE. THEY GRAB FOR THE SUITCASE SIMULTANEOUSLY AND HAVE A TUG OF WAR. THE DAUGHTER WINS THE SUITCASE)

DAUGHTER: I'm going.

DAD: (ON HIS KNEES) No, don't go. You can't go. I need you.

(EXIT DAUGHTER STAGE RIGHT. EXIT EGO STAGE LEFT)

(DAD STILL ON KNEES) No, come back, please, I need you!

(QUIETLY): I love you.

(ENTER EGO AND DAUGHTER)

ALTER EGO: What now?

DAUGHTER: I need to have some fun...meet people...marry someone I love...get a mini skirt...and a stereo system to blow your socks off...

ALTER EGO: In that order?

DAUGHTER: I'm not sure.

ALTER EGO: One thing at a time. Take it easy. What's the one thing you want to do now that you're free?

DAUGHTER: Well I won't feel free until he's off the stage.

(LOOKS AT DAD. HE GETS UP AND EXITS) That's better.

EGO: No.

DAUGHTER: No?

(EGO AND DAUGHTER SMILE AT EACH OTHER, ACCOMPANIED TO THE ORIGINAL PIANO MUSIC OF 'TOOT TOOT TOOTSIE'. THEY PUSH BACK THE ARMCHAIR, TAKE AWAY THE LAMP AND THE SMALL TABLE AND THE DAD'S BELONGINGS, EXCEPT THE REMOTE, WHICH IS PLACED ON THE LARGER TABLE)

ALTER EGO: (RUBBING HANDS TOGETHER) Now that's better. What do you want to do right now? The world is your oyster.

DAUGHTER: Oh. I don't know. Let me think. (PAUSE) I want to lie on a beach in the Islands of Sicily and let a tall dark stranger cover me with sun tan oil.

ALTER EGO: I see.

DAUGHTER: We'd sip champagne on a balcony overlooking the sea...

ALTER EGO: Mmmm?

DAUGHTER: ...and exchange warm caresses...(HUGS HERSELF)

ALTER EGO: It's not like that out there. The sun doesn't always shine in the real world.

DAUGHTER: I want to do a million and one things. So much time has been wasted. I feel so angry. He's ruined my life.

ALTER EGO: No, he hasn't. I know what you want right now.

DAUGHTER: You do?

ALTER EGO: Somewhere to live.

DAUGHTER: Yes, you're right. It's time to be positive. There's such a lot to do for mankind and womankind and we must start straight away.

ALTER EGO: Straight away.

DAUGHTER: Yes straight away.

ALTER EGO: Now!

DAUGHTER: Right now!

ALTER EGO: This very minute!

DAUGHTER: This very second!

ALTER EGO: (PAUSE): Well?

DAUGHTER: Well what?

ALTER EGO: There's such a lot to do for womankind and mankind etc...etc.

DAUGHTER: Yes, well perhaps we'd better have a cup of tea first.

(EXIT DAUGHTER)

ALTER EGO: Er...hang on a sec.

(ENTER DAUGHTER)

Two sugars please.

(EXIT DAUGHTER)

It's okay. I've sorted everything out. I've found a friend that she can go and stay with. I'm deciding how this play is going to go. I'm in charge of everything. I control things round here. No-one else.

(ENTER DAUGHTER)

DAUGHTER: A committee!

ALTER EGO: What?

DAUGHTER: I'm going to form a committee.

ALTER EGO: What for?

DAUGHTER: To get my own back.

ALTER EGO: On who?

DAUGHTER: Dad of course.

ALTER EGO: Where's the people? You need people to form a committee.

DAUGHTER: Well, I've got you.

ALTER EGO: The only person that can see me is you.

DAUGHTER: Well then...er...them. (POINTS TO AUDIENCE)

ALTER EGO: Them?

DAUGHTER: Yes...them.

ALTER EGO: Why do you need a committee?

DAUGHTER: I want to start a pressure group. I want to have the launching meeting in a weeks time...but how do I make them aware of that?

ALTER EGO: Posters.

DAUGHTER: Newsletters and leaflets.

ALTER EGO: We could get the press involved.

DAUGHTER: (NODS): And we could tell them all here and now. (STANDS ON A SOAPBOX) Ladies and gentleman, I'm starting a pressure group, Daughters Against Father Trouble. I intend to curb the males in this life who think they-

ALTER EGO: Daughters Against Father Trouble?

DAUGHTER: Yes, I intend to curb the males in this life who think they own their daughters. So, next week, 7.00 p.m Friday, we have-

ALTER EGO: That's DAFT.

DAUGHTER: (PAUSE) No, it's not. 7.00p.m Friday, we have a meeting then. I do hope you'll all be there.

ALTER EGO: Hang on, you're going to be speaking at this meeting right?

DAUGHTER: Yes.

ALTER EGO: Well, you've got to know what you're talking about.

You must be very knowledgeable on the subject.

DAUGHTER: I am. Take my dad's socks for instance. I know the exact percentage of perspiration they hold and as for their smell...

ALTER EGO: No, I mean they've got to be well known, to add substance to the cause at hand, and attract publicity.

DAUGHTER: I am well known. (LOOKS AT AUDIENCE) They know me.

ALTER EGO: You must have good command of the English language.

DAUGHTER: I'm a walking dictionary, an articulate bomb.

ALTER EGO: But you have to provoke the crowd in order to generate maximum excitement.

DAUGHTER: I can do that. Oh doesn't time fly? It's Friday, 7.00p.m. It's...it's...

ALTER EGO: Crackerjack!

DAUGHTER: I'll crack you in a moment, get the placard. (SHE STANDS ON THE TABLE)

Ladies and gentlemen, regardless of who we are, we've all at, sometime or other, and may still have, a father. These interfering busy bodies stick their noses and quite often their beer bellies into our lives. Unless you are very lucky, parents can make your life sheer hell.

(ENTER ALTER EGO. SHE WALKS UP AND DOWN THE STAGE BRANDISHING A PLACARD WITH THE WORDS D.A.F.T ON IT) Daughters Against Father Trouble protest that we can't do the things we want to while fathers are under the same roof. It's a dictatorship. But possibly the worst thing my dad could have done to me was to treat me like a little girl.

ALTER EGO: Hear, hear.

DAUGHTER: Every other female on this earth is allowed to be a hot blooded sexy woman, but according to my dad, I shouldn't even have sexual reproductive organs. Parents don't own their children, don't they understand that? I reckon we should assassinate their characters in the newspapers and charge them more taxes. That might humble them enough to stop being possessive and just become...decent.

HECKLER: Hang on, hang on. (COMES OUT OF THE AUDIENCE AND WALKS ON STAGE) I've got four kids at home, and another one somewhere in the district...but forget about that for now. I'm a bloody good father and when my kids are sixteen, they can do what they want.

DAUGHTER: Now sir, let me just say that thou art blind to the future.

HECKLER: Yer wha'?

DAUGHTER: Sir, you could be overly possessive without even realising it. You can't plan years ahead. You don't know what you'll be like when they're sixteen, probably some ogre of a father who won't let his kids do anything. Even though you don't believe that now, remember, 'the best laid plans of mice and men'.
HECKLER: PAUSE) Piss off. (DAUGHTER COMES DOWN FROM THE TABLE) What do you know anyway, who do you think you are? (DAUGHTER IS ABOUT TO EXIT)
ALTER EGO: (STANDS IN FRONT OF HECKLER,LIKE A BOUNCER): That's enough. Leave her alone.
DAUGHTER: It's no good, you're wasting your time. He can't hear you. (BEGINS TO WALK AWAY)
HECKLER: That's right, go on, crawl back under your stone. (EXIT HECKLER)
ALTER EGO: Come on, take no notice of him. I'd say you have to try a different approach. What would you say was the most effective for wiping out disease, prevention or cure?
DAUGHTER: I'd say prevention.
ALTER EGO: Exactly...or distraction.
DAUGHTER: What are you getting at?
ALTER EGO: Oh. I see what you mean. (REACHES FOR THE REMOTE ON THE TABLE) You should put the revolution on

hold. I'm planning something. It's called Video Date.

DAUGHTER: What is?

ALTER EGO: (GIVES THE REMOTE CONTROL TO DAUGHTER AND SITS ON THE TABLE) Press the red button. (THE DAUGHTER PRESSES THE RED BUTTON AT ALTER EGO) Hello and welcome to our dating agency. You are now watching a video exclusive to Video Date. I hope you find a man that you would like to date among our collection today. Happy watching.

(ENTER ABACUS WHO EXCHANGES PLACES WITH ALTER EGO)

ABACUS: Er...hello. I enjoy doing most things with a lady. I particularly like doing those wonderful thousand piece jigsaws and carving farm yard animals out of soap. I like walking in the hills, basket weaving and dungeons and dragons.

DAUGHTER: Dungeons and dragons?

ALTER EGO: Role playing.

DAUGHTER: I see. I think.

ABACUS: I also like to count. Some people call me Abacus, it's... one of my nicer nick names. (COUNTS HIS FINGERS AND THUMBS, ONE BY ONE) One, two, three, four, five, six, seven, eight, nine, ten. Oh, oh. I ran out. (HE TAKES HIS

SHOE OFF AND THEN HIS SOCK AND COUNTS THE TOES) eleven, twelve, thirteen, fourteen, fifteen. Oh, oh, ran out! (TAKES OFF OTHER SHOE AND SOCK AND COUNTS) sixteen, seventeen, eighteen, nineteen, twenty. Oh, oh, ran out!

DAUGHTER: (PUTS HER HEAD IN HER HANDS AND GROANS THEN POINTS REMOTE AT ABACUS) I need to fast forward him. (PRESSES BUTTON. THE ACTOR FAST FORWARDS HIS MOVEMENTS TIMES TWO. HE FAST FORWARDS HIMSELF OFF THE STAGE) I think I've seen enough.

ALTER EGO: Oh, but we've only seen one. Give it a chance.

DAUGHTER: Oh. I don't know...

ALTER EGO: There's one more. Just one more.

DAUGHTER: (SIGHS) Okay. One more.

(ENTER CROONER)

CROONER: Hi, I'm an old fashioned guy who is really interested in getting to know a girl. Friendship is so important in a relationship. I'm into the meeting of minds. I want to wine and dine you and eventually fall in love with you. You must have a beautiful attitude and a beautiful mind...and above all...great big tits.

DAUGHTER: Did he just say what I thought he said?

CROONER: Tips! I mean tips. I need advice on a great many things.

ALTER EGO: (GRABS THE REMOTE CONTROL FROM THE DAUGHTER) I think we should do the decent thing. (PRESSES THE RED BUTTON)

(EXIT CROONER WHO FAST FORWARDS OFF THE SET)

DAUGHTER: I think I'll date both of them.

ALTER EGO: What?

DAUGHTER: They would make terrible fathers don't you think, I mean if they had children?

ALTER EGO: You're not still chewing on that bone are you?

DAUGHTER: They could both turn into 'dad' and make someone's life a misery.

ALTER EGO: You can't tar everyone with the same brush.

DAUGHTER: Well that first guy seems needy, that's a bad sign. He would be as clingy as my dad and as for the second, he would be a terrible father to a daughter. He's sexist.

ALTER EGO: Some would say that's an occupational hazard. Look you need to cast that big, fat, greasy chip off your shoulder. Leave the past where it is and look to the future.

DAUGHTER: True. I'd better get ready for these dates.

ALTER EGO: Wait for me! I'm going to be a chaperone and also...

DAUGHTER: What?

ALTER EGO: You're not going out on any date dressed like that.

(EXIT DAUGHTER AND ALTER EGO)

(ENTER DAD WITH HIP FLASK)

DAD: I can't believe she left me. I can't believe I'm all alone. It's true what they say, your biggest fears come true. One of my biggest fears is...the kitchen. It was once so warm and bright and now it's a dark and foreboding place, an undiscovered territory. The pots and pans are all in the cupboards. The bleach and washing up liquid are under the sink. Knifes and forks are in the kitchen drawers. She hides everything! The appliances in there are like futuristic robots, made of cold, unfeeling metal. They won't offer up their secrets of efficiency to me. (NOTICES AUDIENCE) (SUSPICIOUSLY) Don't look at me like that. (NODS) I know what you're thinking, but it's not like that at all. Try walking in my shoes once in a while, or rather slippers. (LOOKS AT HIS SLIPPERS) I could do with a new pair. It's all right for you sat in your cosy little world. Come with your friends have you? Come with your lover, your spouse? Well I've got no-one...but contrary to belief, I'm in control here, I'm in charge. Oh, she'll be back. I'll pull a few strings, help it along. She won't be able to hack it out there in the real world. (PAUSE) I went out in the real world today. I braved the kitchen! (TAKES A SWIG) That's why I'm having this. (TAKES ANOTHER SWIG) My daughter, my only daughter...gone. That's two women I've lost and they can't be replaced. Even a hip can be replaced these days (PAUSE AND THEN TO AUDIENCE) but can they replace a broken heart? (AS THE DAD IS ABOUT TO EXIT, THE DAUGHTER ENTERS, DRESSED TO KILL. THEY WEIGH EACH OTHER UP, LIKE TWO GUNSLINGERS. DAD EXITS)

DAUGHTER: I lost my job. Funny how it happened just after I left my dad. I'm sure, it had nothing to do with him. I'm sure he didn't have a talk to old Fred. I'll be okay. I'll find another job. (EMPTIES POCKETS) I hope it's soon. (PAUSE) He'll be all right without me. He has to be. Guilt is such a negative force. Bending to someone else's will can never be a good thing, I am free from emotional blackmail now. That's true freedom. Freedom to do whatever I like. I can finally get to know what life is all about. I want to know what's out there. It'll take more that a clingy old man to stop me from having a good time. I'll show him! (ENTER EGO)

ALTER EGO: What are we going to do next? (EGO DRAGS THE DAUGHTER TO THE TABLE AND GETS HER TO SIT DOWN) You're meeting these two men aren't you?

DAUGHTER: Who?

ALTER EGO: Those two guys on Video Date.

DAUGHTER: I'm interviewing them.

ALTER EGO: Oh yes, same thing. Now who are you going to meet first, the first idiot or the second idiot?

DAUGHTER: (STANDS UP) I'm not so sure if I need you any more. In fact, I don't need you any more. I'm doing this on my own from now on. It's time. So, I think maybe you should go.

ALTER EGO: But I've got it all worked out!

DAUGHTER: I'm going to work it all out from now on. I want you to leave.

ALTER EGO: But I think...

DAUGHTER: Please leave.

ALTER EGO: Yes, but I...

DAUGHTER: Go!

ALTER EGO: I...

DAUGHTER: Out!

ALTER EGO: (PAUSE) Cow.

(EXIT ALTER EGO)

DAUGHTER: This is it. Finally, it's my turn. Now, where's my note pad? Now, let's see who's first. Oh yes, it's Abacus, the man with the strange counting habit.

(ENTER ABACUS)

ABACUS: Hello.

DAUGHTER: Hello.

ABACUS: Would you like to do this jigsaw?

DAUGHTER: Er...not now. Tell me, would you ever consider becoming a father?

ABACUS: A what?

DAUGHTER: Are you considering having children?

ABACUS: What now? Normally, I'd prefer to do jigsaws.

DAUGHTER: That's not the issue. Now, I'd like to discuss...

ABACUS: I have an excellent thousand piece one at home. It's a scene taken from the Coswolds, a lovely part of Britain, I'm sure you'll agree. It's sitting there at home, just itching to be done. It's left me trembling with anticipation.

DAUGHTER: That's all very nice but would you ever consider fathering a child?

ABACUS: This is all going a little bit too fast for me. (HE OPENS UP HIS JIGSAW AND STARTS COUNTING THE PIECES) One, two, three, four, five, six, seven...

DAUGHTER: Why am I wasting my time on him for? He's not a danger to society.

ABACUS: eight, nine, ten, eleven, twelve, thirteen, fourteen, fifteen, sixteen...

DAUGHTER: Goodbye.

ABACUS: What? Is the date over...already?

DAUGHTER: Yes.

ABACUS: Oh. Seventeen, eighteen, nineteen, twenty...

DAUGHTER: Please leave and take the jigsaw with you.

(EXIT ABACUS DESPONDENTLY)

DAUGHTER: What a weird man. I just can't imagine going through life doing jigsaws...and counting...so I'll cross him off...now! I hope the next one is better. I need a man who understands me, who has time for me, a man who is interested in my finer feelings, a man with charisma.

(ENTER CROONER, WITH A MICROPHONE. HE SINGS A JAZZED UP VERSION OF 'ANYTIME' BY HERBERT LAWSON. HE DANCES WTH THE DAUGHTER AND HOLDS HER IN A DRAMATIC EMBRACE AT THE END OF THE SONG. THEY ARE SUPPOSED TO RETAIN THE POSE, BUT HE CAN'T HOLD HER IN THAT POSITION FOR TOO LONG AND HE DROPS HER SLOWLY. HE FALLS ON TOP OF HER AND THE DAD ENTERS. THE COUPLE SCRAMBLE TO THEIR FEET AND HOLD EACH OTHER. THE DAD HAS HIS ADDRESSES THE AUDIENCE).

DAD: (TO THE AUDIENCE) I've got this situation under control. (STUMBLES) It doesn't matter if I end up on my back...as long as she doesn't! But it's okay, I'm pulling the strings. (TAKES A SWIG FROM HIS HIP FLASK. Want to join me in a drink? (PAUSE) or is it that you don't fancy supping with an old bugger like me? I should have let her come the pub with me when I had the chance. Now she's gone, in a puff of smoke. Whoooosh! (ENTER ALTER EGO. TO AUDIENCE).

ALTER EGO: Is it up to me, should I be the one handing out advice, because let's face it, I've always been pretty good at that kind of thing. I'm at the proverbial wheel of this auto mobile. I can control her mind. I could just snap my fingers and everything would go the way that I just want it to, but (LAUGHS) you know, this is a touchy subject. I mean the daughter will do what the daughter will do, what she has to do. Like all daughters, like all sons, like all humans, how else would we learn from our mistakes? So I say...go for it.

(DAD TAKES DAUGHTER BY THE HAND AND PULLS HER FROM THE CROONER)

DAD: She's mine.

DAUGHTER: What it is, you see, is the cotton wool thing.

DAD: Cotton wool?

DAUGHTER: Wrapped up for too long, you go numb.

DAD: Keeping you safe, that's all.

DAUGHTER: Safe and sorry.

DAD: Safe. My little girl, safe.

DAUGHTER: Dad?

DAD: Bruise. Bruise easily once you go out there.

DAUGHTER: Dad?

DAD: Too many bad men in the world.

DAUGHTER: Dad?

DAD: What?

DAUGHTER: Give it a rest. (SHE PULLS AWAY FROM DAD)

CROONER: Don't move!

DAUGHTER: What?

CROONER: Don't move one inch.

DAUGHTER: Why not?

CROONER: I see...I see...an angelic light behind you.

DAUGHTER & ALTER EGO: Really?

CROONER: You're radiant.

(DAUGHTER AND ALTER EGO LAUGH)

CROONER: No, no, I'm serious. You look like someone who needs love, who dreams of love. Do you dream of love? (THE CROONER TAKES THE DAUGHTERS HAND) You deserve love. I can give you love. If you asked for the moon...I'd give it to you.

DAUGHTER: Na.

CROONER: Yeah.

DAUGHTER: Na.

CROONER: Yeah. Straight up.

(ENTER DAD, ENTER ALTER EGO, ACCOMPANIED TO 'ENTRANCE TO THE GLADIATORS' FAIRGROUND MUSIC. DAD, CROONER AND ALTER EGO BECOME STATUES AND FORM A HUMAN TRIANGLE. ALTER EGO WEARS A HEADSCARF, HOLDS A CRYSTAL BALL AND BECOMES THE GYPSY. THE DAD WEARS A BOWLER HAT AND BECOMES THE SWINDLER.

THE DAUGHTER INSPECTS EACH STATUE, GIGGLING AND DANCING HER WAY FROM ONE TO THE OTHER. AS SHE INSPECTS THE CROONER, THE GYSPY TEMPTS HER WITH THE BALL. SHE POINTS TO IT AND THEN TO THE CROONER.

CROONER JUGGLES. ALTER EGO TAKES OFF THE SCARF AND PUTS IT ROUND THE DAUGHTERS NECK. SHE PUTS ON A SHORT FUR COAT AND IS NOW THE PROSTITUTE).

SWINDLER: Roll up! Roll up! Pay a pound and win a fiver!

Choose the cup that hides the pea! You sir, you madam? Would you like a go? It's easy.

(DAD/SWINDLER NOTICES THE DAUGHTER)

Roll up! Pay a pound, win a fiver! You madam, (DAUGHTER LOOKS BEHIND HER, THEN POINTS TO HERSELF) Yes you? Would you like to take a chance? (PAUSE) Chose the cup that hides the pea.

(THE DAUGHTER PAYS A POUND AND HAS TWO GOS AT FINDING THE PEA BUT LOSES. THE CROONER AND PROSTITUTE ARE CHATTING. THE DAUGHTER WALKS AWAY FROM THE SWINDLER BUT HE PULLS HER BACK).

SWINDLER: One pound admission fee.

(DAUGHTER HANDS OVER YET ANOTHER POUND)

What a sucker! I mean...what a lovely girl! Come back soon.

('ENTRANCE TO THE GLADIATORS' FADES AND IS REPLACED BY CREEPY MUSIC BOX TUNE, 'COME OUT AND PLAY' BY DESPERATE MEASUREZ. THE CROONER FLUTTERS MONEY UNDER PROSTITUTE'S NOSE. SHE FOLLOWS HIM AND GRABS THE MONEY. THEY DANCE BRIEFLY. THE PROSTITUTE FLUTTERS MONEY UNDER DAUGHTERS NOSE. SHE FOLLOWS, DISORIENTATED. PROSTITUTE LEADS THE DAUGHTER TO THE CROONER.

THE DAUGHTER AND CROONER SLOW DANCE, IN THE STYLE OF MUSIC BOX DANCERS. THE CROONER GRABS AT HER CLOTHING AND PUSHES HER TO THE FLOOR. HE EXITS. THE DAUGHTER IS NOW SITTING ON THE FLOOR IN SHOCK. THE SWNDLER/DAD PUTS HIS HAT ON HER HEAD AND EXITS. PROSTITUTE THROWS HER COAT AT DAUGHTER AND EXITS. THE MUSIC STOPS. ENTER ABACUS)

ABACUS: Are you all right?

DAUGHTER: Not really.

(HE COUNTS HER FINGERS THEN HELPS HER UP)

ABACUS: Any broken bones?

DAUGHTER: Don't think so?

ABACUS: Dizzy?

DAUGHTER: Only with disappointment.

ABACUS: I'll see you home. Do you live nearby?

DAUGHTER: I'm fine. You're that nutcase...I mean that nice man on Video Date.

ABACUS: (COUNTS HIS FINGERS) There's no need to humour me.

DAUGHTER: Thank you for helping me. I'm okay. I can walk.

ABACUS: As long as you're sure.

DAUGHTER: Taxi!

(EXIT DAUGHTER, STAGE RIGHT. ABACUS IS ABOUT TO ENTER STAGE LEFT WHEN HE NOTICES THE SCARF SHE WAS WEARING IS NOW ON THE FLOOR. HE PICKS IT UP) Oh, wait, your scarf...(SIGHS AND HURRIES AFTER DAUGHTER, EXIT STAGE RIGHT)

(EGO AND DAD ENTER AND TALK INDEPENDENTLY OF EACH OTHER)

DAD: I have everything under control.

ALTER EGO: Me too.

DAD: I've got her on a lead. I admit its a longer lead than what you'd expect, but it's still a lead.

ALTER EGO: I thought I was in her head.

DAD: She'll find her way home, just like dogs do.

ALTER EGO: That's cats. Cats find their way home.

DAD: Daughters, cats, dogs, people...whatever they are, they can find their way home. Let them have a party, get into trouble and burn themselves out.

ALTER EGO: Then crawl back to the safety of the gilded cage.

DAD: A sweet prison though, a very sweet prison.

(EXIT DAD)

(ENTER DAUGHTER)

ALTER EGO: Two down. Millions to go.

DAUGHTER: What?

ALTER EGO: Well come on, admit it. It's silly. How many fathers and would be fathers are there in the world?

DAUGHTER: Quite a few.

ALTER EGO: There are good apples and bad apples. You just got a bad apple.

DAUGHTER: Dad's not a bad apple. He's just an apple that nobody wants.

(DAUGHTER SITS DOWN AND PUTS HER HEAD IN HER HANDS)

ALTER EGO: What's wrong?

DAUGHTER: I'm depressed, frustrated and discontented.

ALTER EGO: So everything's normal then?

DAUGHTER: No, it's that man before, the one I went off with.

ALTER EGO: You mean The Crooner?

DAUGHTER: Was that his name?

ALTER EGO: He modelled himself on some 1950's singer...his name escapes me right now.

DAUGHTER: Well, whatever his name was, he slapped me onto a plate, held me down with his fork, stuck his knife into the flesh and...carved.

ALTER EGO: (PULLS A FACE): I take it there was no dessert.

DAUGHTER: Like a fruit sundae without the fruit.

ALTER EGO: Oh dear.

DAUGHTER: He didn't make me feel like a woman at all. When he'd had his fill, he left an empty plate and he didn't even bother to set his knife and fork straight.

ALTER EGO: We're all consumers. Just because we drink some milk, it doesn't mean we want the glass afterwards.

DAUGHTER: I thought he'd have wanted the glass.

ALTER EGO: Life is all about disillusion. It's how we grow.

DAUGHTER: Maybe so, but I miss a man about the place.

ALTER EGO: Not your dad surely?

DAUGHTER: (SHRUGS): I miss the toothpaste being squeezed in the middle...and what I'd give to go into a bathroom again where the toilet seat is left up. You're usually the one who has all the answers. What do I do now?

ALTER EGO: It's up to you. You're on your own. Only you can decide your future.

(DAUGHTER MOVES UPSTAGE LEFT, EGO MOVES UPSTAGE RIGHT, THEN EXITS)

(ENTER ABACUS)

DAUGHTER: Oh hello, what are you doing here?

ABACUS: You forgot your scarf.

DAUGHTER: Oh...er...thank you. How did you know where to find me?

ABACUS: You got into a taxi and then I got a taxi and said, 'Follow that taxi'

DAUGHTER: You did all that just to return a scarf? That's very kind of you.

ABACUS: You look sad.

DAUGHTER: (LAUGHS) Really? I'm not.

ABACUS: Yes, you are. I notice that about people, whether they're happy or sad, or angry, or whatever.

DAUGHTER: Well, that's sweet, but (SIGHS) I'm really okay.

ABACUS: That's the upside of being someone like me. I have empathy but it turns me upside down and inside out, so I do jigsaws to relax me, and that's the downside because when I mention jigsaws and all the other stuff I'm into, people turn away.

DAUGHTER: Oh. (LOOKS SAD AND NODS): I know what it's like to get rejected.

(ABACUS TAKES HER HAND AND BEGINS TO COUNT HER FINGERS OUT LOUD AND THEN HE COUNTS THE OTHER HAND. THEN HE TRIES TO TAKE OFF HER SHOE AND SHE FALLS ON THE FLOOR. HE COUNTS BOTH SETS

OF TOES)

ABACUS: Oh, oh. I've ran out!

(ABACUS STARTS TO COUNT PEOPLE IN THE AUDIENCE)

ABACUS: Oh, Oh. I've ran out!

DAUGHTER: Stop it! Stop it!

(ABACUS STARTS COUNTING EVERYTHING IN SIGHT. DAUGHTER GRABS HIS HANDS AND STOPS HIM) Why do you do that?

ABACUS (PAUSE) I don't know. No-one's ever asked me that before.

DAUGHTER: Well, I'm asking you now.

ABACUS: I think...I think it's because I'm nervous.

DAUGHTER: You get nervous a lot don't you?

ABACUS: Yes.

DAUGHTER: So why are you nervous now?

ABACUS: (PAUSE) Because...because I like you.

DAUGHTER: Well, I've been liked before and it hasn't turned out so well.

ABACUS: I'm not like the others.

DAUGHTER: I can see that. (ABACUS STARTS COUNTING THINGS AGAIN)

What would make you stop being nervous?

ABACUS: I don't know. Maybe if you liked me, which I know you don't, which why I'm nervous. No-one understands me.

DAUGHTER: No-one understands me either.

ABACUS: We have something in common.

DAUGHTER: Yes.

(ABACUS PUTS THE SHOES BACK THE ON DAUGHTER'S FEET)

Now that's better. Thank you.

ABACUS: Would you...would you go out to dinner with me, sometime?

DAUGHTER: And if I said no you'd start to count wouldn't you?

ABACUS: Like my life depended on it.

DAUGHTER: (LAUGHS) You're funny.

ABACUS: Yes, people laugh at me a lot.

DAUGHTER: Oh, I'm not laughing at you. (PAUSE) I'd love to go out with you.

ABACUS: You'd really come out with me?

DAUGHTER: Yes. Why don't we go out now, for a coffee or something? (PAUSE) You won't start counting when we're there though, will you?

ABACUS: I'll try not to.

(EXIT DAUGHTER AND ABACUS)

(ENTER DAD)

DAD: I'd do anything to see her scowling face again and to hear the awful music she used to play, to smell the perfume that used to choke me and to eat a decent meal.

Am I the lonely old man that you see in the pub on his own, staring glassy eyed into his pint of beer and wanting to dive in? Why is he there? Ever thought why? I used to look at them once and pity them. It's a blow to realise that the tables have turned and now they're all looking at me. Don't feel sorry for me though. No-one feels sorry for me, no-one!

(EXIT DAD)

(BOTH THE DAUGHTER AND THE ALTER EGO GO TO THE MIRROR FRAME. THE STROBE COMES ON. AFTER SOME CHOREOGRAPHED SIMULTANEOUS MOVEMENTS, THE DAUGHTER, ALTER EGO AND ABACUS RETURN THE SMALL TABLE AND THE ARMCHAIR TO THE STAGE. DAUGHTER EXITS WITH ABACUS. ALTER EGO SITS ON THE TABLE, OUT OF BREATH)

ALTER EGO: (GASPS): We can't stop that friend stroke foe, we call time. (GASPS): It goes on, for the worse and for the better. Daughters have a second childhood, teenage hood and womanhood all at once. Twelve months on and things will never

be the same again. Thank God. (PAUSE) It's time for me to go.
(WEDDING SCENE BETWEEN ABACUS & DAUGHTER)
(EXIT ALTER EGO)
(ENTER DAD WHO IS PLEASANTLY SURPRISED TO SEE THE RETURN OF HIS CHAIR. HE SITS DOWN, CARESSING THE CHAIR LOVINGLY. ENTER DAUGHTER)

DAUGHTER: Dad...I...

DAD: Slut.

DAUGHTER: Is that so?

DAD: Yes.

DAUGHTER: And men aren't I suppose?

DAD: Of course not. How can they be?

(ENTER CROONER)

DAUGHTER: (ADDRESSES CROONER): Slut. Dirty slut. You dirty, filthy, slutty, hussy, slaggy whore.

CROONER: (PAUSES. SMUGLY CROSSES ARMS) It doesn't have the same effect somehow does it?

DAUGHTER: Oh, it will. One day. I'll make sure of it.

CROONER: I'm a stud.

DAUGHTER: Why can't I be the stud?

DAD: Wash your mouth out with soap!

CROONER: You can't be a stud because it's just not done. You're the slut. I'm the stud. I'm looked up to for my sexuality. You're looked down on for yours. That's the way it is, the way it's always going to be...doll.

DAUGHTER: We'll see. Thanks for the lousy time in bed...stud.
(SHE GRABS HIM IN THE GROIN AREA ON THE WORD 'STUD' AND THEN WIPES HER HANDS)
(CROONER CRINGES AND CROSSES HIS LEGS. CROONER EXITS, WITH DIFFICULTY)
Right, what's next. Oh yes, if you'll excuse me for a moment...
(EXIT DAUGHTER. ENTER DAUGHTER WITH A SUITCASE AND A BABY DOLL WRAPPED IN A BLANKET)
Here you are dad, this is for you.
(HANDS THE BABY TO DAD)
DAD: What? Whose baby is it?
DAUGHTER: Why mine of course. (STARTS PACKING) Now, listen carefully, she needs feeding every four hours.(WAVES HAND IN FRONT OF FACE) ...and she definitely needs changing now. But don't worry, you'll get used to the smell of nappies...eventually. Oh and she might keep you awake at night. I'm going on holiday with my lovely husband...who doesn't count things any more...well not much, and when I come back, she'd better be all nice and clean and happy. Just like you eh dad?

(SHE PINCHES HIS CHEEK) You look after her, the way I've looked after you. Now maybe you'll know what it's like to help the helpless. See you dad.
(EXIT DAUGHTER)
DAD: No, don't go. Come back!
(THE DAD PANICS AT FIRST THEN LOOKS DOWN, SMILES AND GENTLY ROCKS THE BABY)
Daddy's little girl.

(LIGHTS FADE)

CURTAIN

www.ingramcontent.com/pod-product-compliance
Lightning Source LLC
Chambersburg PA
CBHW071824170526
45167CB00003B/1406